**Dan
De**

For most of his life, Daniel had lived in Babylon. It wasn't his home, and the people there did not serve God. But Daniel prayed three times a day. He did everything he could to live the way God wanted him to.

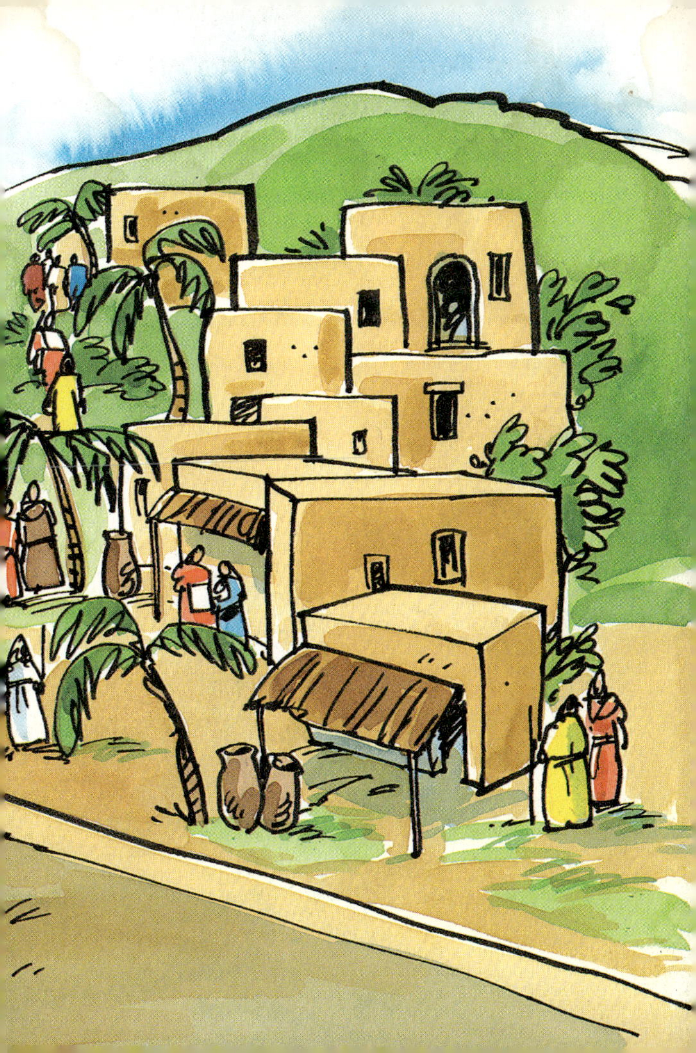

Daniel knew that he needed God's help in everything he did, especially as Daniel's job was to help King Darius look after his vast empire.

Daniel was so good at his job that one day the king said, "Daniel is so trustworthy and reliable, I will put him in charge of my whole empire!"

The other leaders who had been helping to rule the empire were not pleased. They were so jealous that they started plotting to kill Daniel.

"But we cannot kill Daniel ourselves," whispered one of them. "We'd get caught."

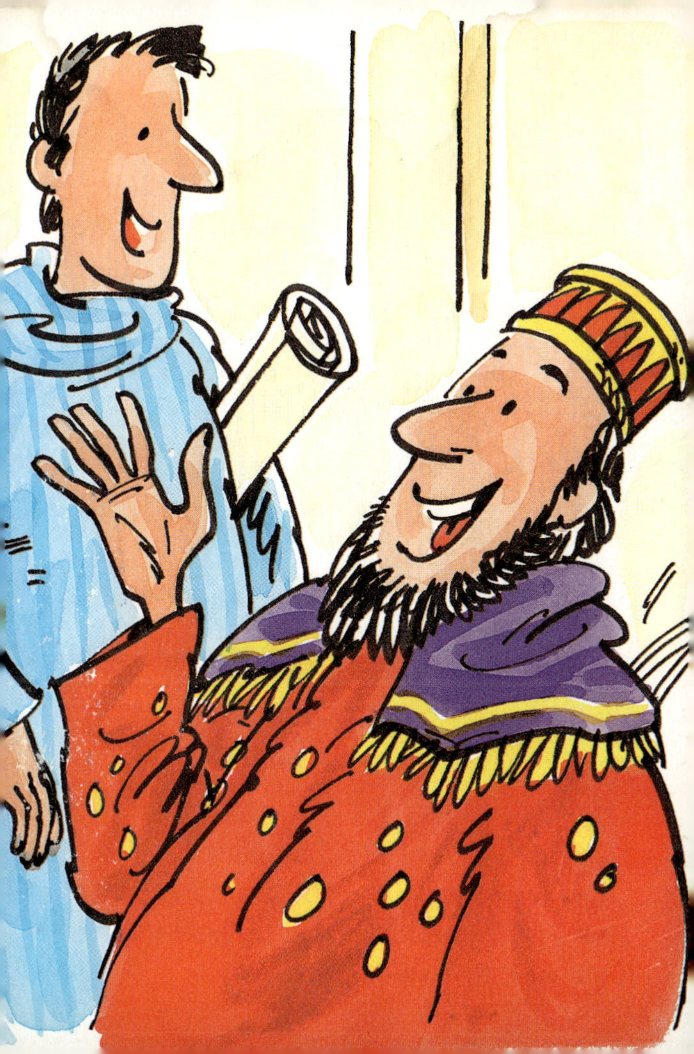

"I've got an idea!" said another.

He explained his crafty plan and the others all agreed. It was a brilliant idea and together they raced to the palace.

"King Darius, may you live for ever!" they said. "You are such a wonderful and marvellous king we think everyone should pray only to you!"

The king blushed with pride.

"In fact," the leader continued, "if anyone is caught praying to anyone else they should be thrown into the lions' den!"

The king agreed with their suggestions and a few moments later a new law was made:
For the next thirty days people must pray only to King Darius. Anyone found praying to someone else will be thrown to the lions.

Daniel and the Den of Lions

Open up this re-usable picture. Decorate it with the stickers in this book!

Now use your stickers!

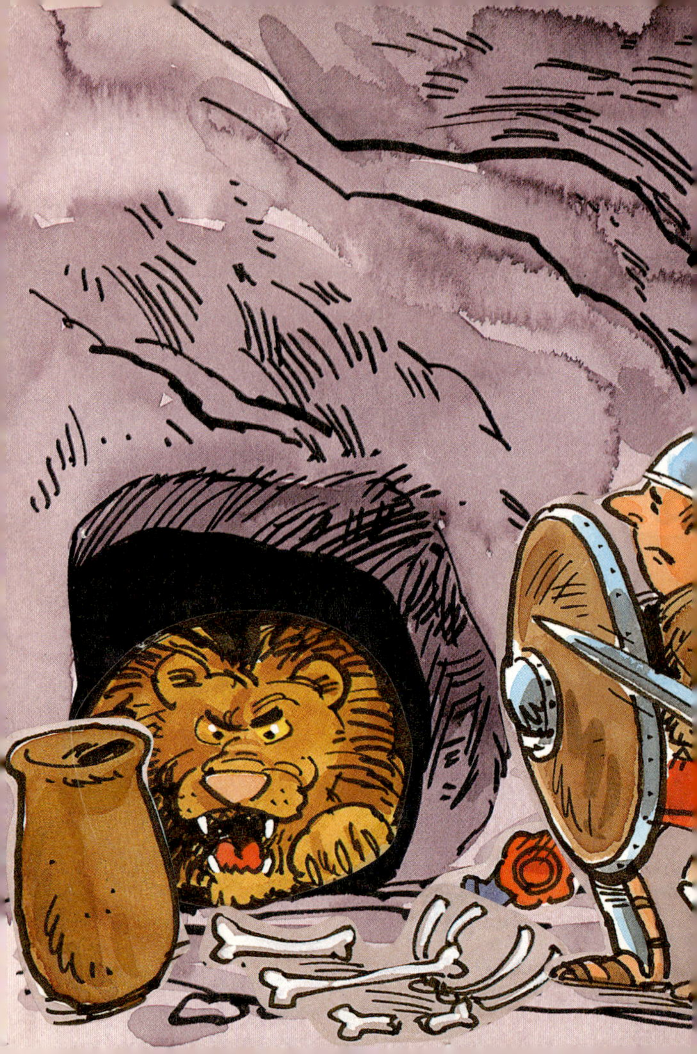

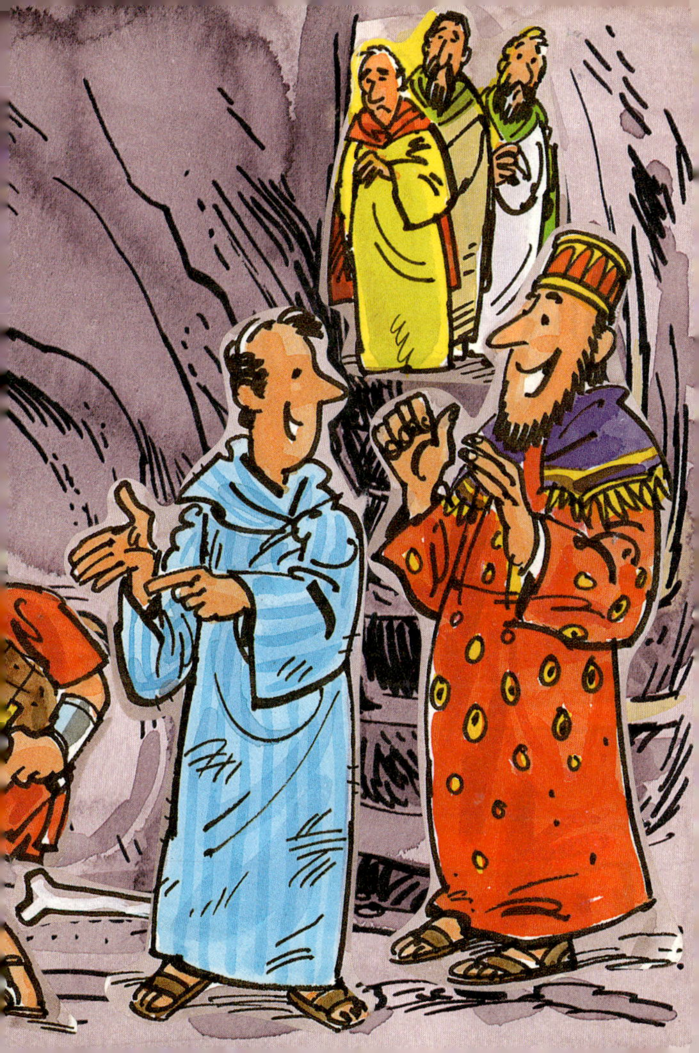

Have fun with your Collect-a-Bible-Story!

1. Read the whole story.
2. Carefully remove the re-usable stickers.
3. Complete the picture. Display it in your room!

Collect the whole series!

Every Collect-a-Bible-Story comes with re-usable stickers and a picture for you to decorate. Make sure you get each one!

The leaders rubbed their hands with glee and off they raced to Daniel's house.

Three times a day Daniel would go to his room to pray. Often he left his window open, and people could see – and sometimes hear – Daniel talking to God.

As soon as he began to pray, his door burst open and the band of jealous leaders tumbled in.

Within minutes Daniel was dragged in front of King Darius.

"We caught Daniel praying to God when he should have been praying to you!" the leaders exclaimed.

"Well," said the king, who liked Daniel very much, "I'll let him off this time."

"You can't do that!" snarled one of the leaders. "The law cannot be changed!"

The king was horrified. He summoned his best lawyers and they studied their scrolls. But it was true: the law could not be changed. Daniel would have to be thrown to the lions.

With tears in his eyes King Darius watched Daniel being thrown into the den full of hungry lions. A huge stone was rolled across the entrance. The king watched as the door was closed. Then, with a very heavy heart, he added his own seal-mark to the stone door. Only Daniel's God could rescue him now.

King Darius returned to his palace. He did not sleep a wink. He knew he had been tricked. And by now Daniel would be dead...

The following morning King Darius stood by the stone door of the lions' den. He felt very sad. Suddenly, he heard a voice from inside!

"O King, live for ever!" said Daniel. "God sent his angel and the lions haven't touched me."

King Darius was overjoyed and immediately ordered the den to be opened. Daniel was lifted out. There was not a mark on him. God had looked after Daniel.

King Darius turned to his soldiers. "Go and fetch those evil rascals who tricked me into putting Daniel in the lions' den," he said. "And from now on, there is a new law. Everyone must love and serve Daniel's God, the true and living God, who has the power to save even from the mouths of lions."